Working for our Future

Healthy Mothers

Judith Anderson

In Association with Christian Aid

christian aid — We believe in life before death

FRANKLIN WATTS
LONDON·SYDNEY

First published in 2007 by
Franklin Watts
338 Euston Road
London NW1 3BH

Franklin Watts Australia
Level 17/207 Kent Street
Sydney NSW 2000
Copyright © Franklin Watts 2007

Editor: Jeremy Smith
Art director: Jonathan Hair
Design: Rita Storey
Artwork: John Alston

Produced in association with Christian Aid.

Franklin Watts would like to thank Christian Aid for their help with this title, in particular for allowing permission to use the information concerning Heidy and Marta which is © Christian Aid.

Picture credits: Alamy: 1, 3b, 3c, 10t, 12, 13b, 14, 17, 19, 23t, 25b, 27t. Christian Aid: 3br, 9, 11, 21b, 22b, 23b, 25t, 26t. Children in Crisis/Jinpa: 20. istockphoto.com: 4-5, 6-7, 13t, 16, 21, 22t, 24, 28-29. James Elder: 3bc, 15, 18, 26b, 27b. World Food Programme: 8.

Every attempt has been made to clear copyright. Should there by any inadvertent omission please apply to the publisher for rectification.

Dewey Classification 362.7

ISBN: 978 0 7496 7349 9

Printed in China

Franklin Watts is a division of Hachette Children's Books, an Hachette Livre UK company.

The Millennium Development Goals

In 2000, government leaders agreed on eight goals to help build a better, fairer world in the 21st century. These goals include getting rid of extreme poverty, fighting child mortality and disease, promoting education, gender equality and maternal health and ensuring sustainable development.

The aim of this series is to look at the problems these goals address, show how they are being tackled at local level and relate them to the experiences of children around the world.

Contents

The Cast

In this book, follow the stories of these adults and children from around the world, all affected by disease and poverty in different ways.

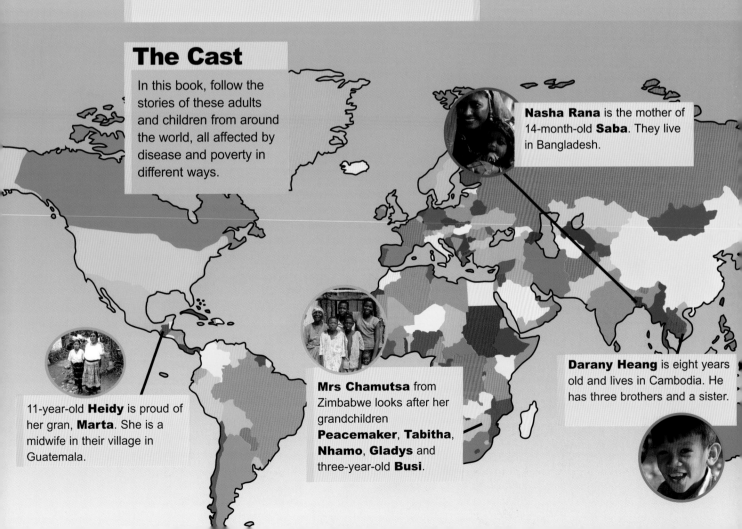

Nasha Rana is the mother of 14-month-old **Saba**. They live in Bangladesh.

11-year-old **Heidy** is proud of her gran, **Marta**. She is a midwife in their village in Guatemala.

Mrs Chamutsa from Zimbabwe looks after her grandchildren **Peacemaker**, **Tabitha**, **Nhamo**, **Gladys** and three-year-old **Busi**.

Darany Heang is eight years old and lives in Cambodia. He has three brothers and a sister.

Babies need mothers

Babies need lots of special care as they can do very little for themselves. They rely on their mothers for milk and a safe place to sleep. They also need to be washed and they need to have their nappies changed. Babies also need plenty of cuddles!

When you were a baby, you relied on your mother to take care of you. Ask her how she did this. What did you drink? What did you eat? Where did you sleep? ▶

Baby food

Milk is the best food for newborn babies. Many mothers feed their babies on breast milk, which has all the nutrients a growing baby needs. Other babies are fed on formula milk, which is similar to breast milk. Mothers usually feed their babies different types of food such as porridge and mashed vegetables when they are a few months old.

◀ When they are first born, babies are fed on just milk, but after a few months they can start eating solid food.

Keeping things clean

Young babies pick up infections more quickly than older children. Their bodies haven't yet grown strong enough to fight off illness. So good hygiene is essential. Babies rely on their mothers to make sure that your drinking water, feeding bottles and pacifiers were completely clean and free of germs.

A baby's bottle must be kept sterile because germs can cause diseases that can be very harmful to babies.

Protection against disease

Many mothers take their babies for immunisations when they are just a few months old. An immunisation is an injection or a medicine that stops you from getting certain diseases such as measles or tuberculosis or whooping cough. Babies cannot be immunised against every disease, but a terrible disease called polio has now disappeared from almost every country in the world because of immunisation.

Immunising babies and chidren when they are young protects them from catching serious diseases.

? **Why do you think very young babies are at particular risk from infection and disease?**

New mothers

New mothers need to stay healthy too. A well-balanced, plentiful diet is important both before and after the baby is born. Regular appointments with a midwife, nurse or doctor mean that any health problems can be spotted and treated as quickly as possible. A healthy mother is more likely to have a healthy baby.

A healthy diet should consist of plenty of fresh fruit and vegetables; pasta, rice or potatoes; dairy products such as milk, yoghurt or cheese and some meat, fish, beans, lentils or eggs. ▶

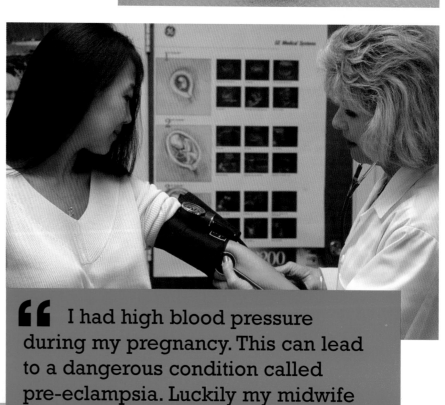

A visit to a clinic

Women in the developed world often visit a health clinic during and after pregnancy. They may see a nurse, or a doctor, or a midwife (an expert in pregnancy and birth). They will have their blood pressure checked, their weight monitored and they may have an ultrasound examination to make sure that their unborn baby is comfortable and well. When it is time for the baby to be born, a midwife or a doctor will be on hand to take care of them.

Susan, a new mother, says:

" I had high blood pressure during my pregnancy. This can lead to a dangerous condition called pre-eclampsia. Luckily my midwife spotted the problem in time. "

Eating well

A woman who is pregnant needs to eat a variety of healthy foods in order to pass on essential nutrients to her baby growing in her womb. Once the baby is born, a good diet helps the mother build up her strength and helps her produce enough breast milk to feed her baby. Many new mothers are given special advice on diet by health visitors and nutrition experts. This gives their babies the very best start in life.

❝ My mum ate loads of fruit and vegetables when she was expecting my baby sister. She said she needed the extra vitamins. ❞

Kieran, aged 9

◄ A baby drinks breast milk from her mother.

❓ Ask a new mother how she looked after herself and her baby during her pregnancy.

Mothers and babies at risk

Most women in rich, developed countries are looked after by a trained midwife when they have a baby. They have access to health clinics and hospitals. Their newborn babies receive expert care. But mothers and babies in other parts of the world are not so fortunate. Two million babies die within the first 24 hours of life each year. Most of them are born in poorer, developing countries.

A preventable tragedy?

Every year more than half a million women die due to problems in pregnancy and childbirth. All but a tiny proportion of these deaths occur in developing countries where mothers are often as young as 15 and where there is a lack of midwives and hospitals. Most newborn baby deaths are caused by infections, complications during birth or because they are born too small and weak to survive. The first hours, days and weeks of a baby's life are critical, but many do not receive proper healthcare during this vulnerable period.

" For most children in the developing world, the most dangerous day of their lives is the day they are born. **"**

Jasmine Whitbread of the charity Save the Children.

Having a baby in Guatemala

In Guatemala, most villages don't have a doctor or a midwife. Lots of mothers and babies die because they don't get the care they need. Women who live near Heidy's grandmother Marta are more fortunate because Marta is a midwife. However, she still has to deal with many problems.

Marta says:

❝ I have no thermometer and no blood pressure equipment. I have to use my eyes and my touch to see if a woman is ill or well. ❞

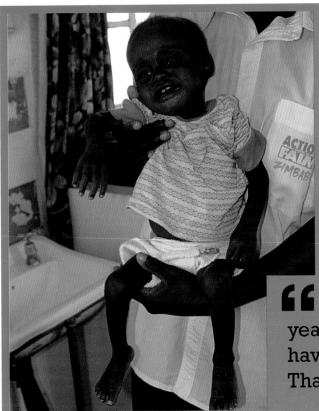

Asirene Magalasi lives in Malawi. Her son Mphatso (left) is just two months old and is suffering from malnutrition. She says:

❝ We've grown no food since last year. I was eating once a day. I didn't have enough food so I had no milk. That's why he [Mphatso] got sick. ❞

 What would help baby Mphatso to get well?

Disease and hunger

For many children, the struggle to survive continues throughout their early years. In the poorest, least developed countries, one child in six dies before its fifth birthday. Most of these children die from lung infections, diarrhoea, diseases such as measles and malaria, or from malnutrition (hunger).

 Women collect purified water from a lake in India. Without clean water people risk catching serious diseases.

Diarrhoea

People get diarrhoea after drinking dirty water, eating contaminated food or by failing to wash their hands after going to the toilet. It is rarely a serious illness for a well-fed child. However, for malnourished children, it can be fatal. Their bodies become dangerously dehydrated – especially in a hot climate – and without clean water to drink or proper medical care they cannot recover.

Malaria

Malaria is a serious disease spread by the bite of mosquitoes in hot, humid countries. Children under the age of five are particularly at risk. One of the best ways to reduce the danger is to sleep under a simple bed-net as the mosquitoes are only active at night. Yet many children in developing countries don't have a bed-net.

Mosquito nets in a bedroom in Ethiopia.

Measles

Measles used to be a very common disease. Nowadays it has almost disappeared from some parts of the world due to immunisation. Yet in those countries where routine immunisation has not taken place, it is still a very real threat and 300,000 children still die from complications caused by measles every year.

Lack of food

Malnourished children are much more likely to become seriously ill with lung infections, malaria and diarrhoea. Yet when they are sick, they can no longer eat what little food they have. So it is even more difficult for them to recover.

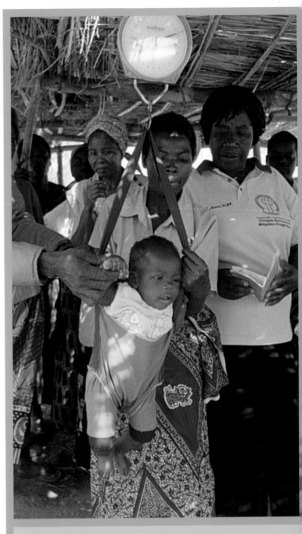

Nurse Kaoza works at the child survival clinic (above and left) in Malawi.

❝ Last month we had 3,000 malnourished children in our clinics. We send any severely malnourished children on to the hospital in Zomba. They come back after about a month there, but often they become badly ill again (because their families have no food). ❞

? A malnourished child is more likely to die from diseases such as diarrhoea and malaria. Why is this?

Why are so many dying?

Disease, infection and a lack of food and clean water are the main reasons why so many mothers and children are dying. Not enough nurses, midwives, clinics, hospitals and medicines is another reason. So too is a lack of awareness about health issues and hygiene. And all these reasons are linked by one huge problem: poverty.

The problem of poverty

Poverty means that people don't have enough money to buy food and medicines. It means that communities cannot afford to install taps and water pipes to ensure a clean water supply. It means that no one can afford to train and pay health experts such as midwives. It means that parents cannot afford to immunise their children against diseases such as measles.

Lack of awareness

Parents in some countries don't have enough information about good diet, or basic hygiene, or how to use a bed net to stop the mosquitoes that carry malaria from biting their children. A virus called HIV that can lead to a deadly disease called AIDS affects a lot of mothers and children, especially in parts of Africa, yet many people have not been educated in how to prevent HIV from spreading. Lack of knowledge means deadly diseases spread very quickly.

Nasha Rana lives in Bangladesh with her 14-month old daughter, Saba. When Saba became sick, Nasha struggled to find enough money to pay for the treatment her daughter needed.

" Nasha used to be very sick with lots of coughs and fever. I spent a lot of money for treatments and doctors. Even so, the nearest doctor is a one hour walk away. **"**

Lack of resources

A mother with HIV/AIDS can pass the disease on to her unborn child. It is possible to prevent this by giving the mother special drugs called anti-retrovirals just before the baby is born, then giving the baby the same drugs for the first two or three months of its life. However, it is estimated that only 10 per cent of pregnant women who need these drugs for their unborn babies have access to them.

A doctor in his surgery in Nigeria. He does his best for his patients but he has only a limited supply of drugs.

Darany Heang

Darany Heang lives in a remote part of Cambodia with his parents and brothers and sister. His parents first noticed that he could not see very well when he was two years old, but they did not think his problem was serious. They did not know that their son's poor sight was caused by a lack of vitamin A in his diet. We get vitamin A mainly from dairy products, eggs and dark green and deep orange fruits and vegetables.

Darany Heang says:

❝ Once it is dark, I cannot see. **❞**

? **Why do you think Darany Heang's parents were unaware of the cause of his poor sight?**

Too many orphans

Sickness and disease affects whole families – not just those who are ill. When parents become sick they cannot work, and in countries where the government does not provide help this often means they cannot afford to feed their children. The situation is especially difficult for orphans. With no one to take care of them they are likely to become malnourished and ill themselves.

HIV/AIDS

HIV/AIDS is particularly devastating for families. It often affects both parents and in some parts of the world the disease is so widespread that millions of orphans are now growing up alone or looking after their younger brothers and sisters in extreme poverty. Already, 15 million children have been orphaned by AIDS.

Life in Zimbabwe

In Zimbabwe, a poor African country with very few resources, more than 70 children are orphaned every day. If they are lucky they are brought up by family members, but many end up in an orphanage.

Orphaned children in Zimbabwe. Their parents all died of AIDS.

A grandmother's story

The five Chamutsa children live in the village of Murambinda, in Zimbabwe. Their parents have died from AIDS related illnesses and they are looked after by their 84-year-old grandmother, Mrs Chamutsa. In Zimbabwe, despite the difficult living conditions, many orphans are cared for by grandparents or uncles and aunts and Mrs Chamutsa does her best but it is not easy.

Mrs Chamutsa does her best for Peacemaker, Tabitha, Nhamo, Gladys and three-year-old Busi, but she says that motherhood should be for younger women:

❝ There are many grandparents who are looking after children because of AIDS. Many cannot keep their children in school, or in good health. Many just don't cope. And things get harder every day. **❞**

? **Why does Mrs Chamutsa say that motherhood should be for younger women?**

The Millennium Development Goals

In the year 2000 the world's leaders met at the United Nations and agreed a set of eight goals that would help to make the world a better, fairer place in the 21st century. Goals four and five focus on the health of mothers and children, but all eight goals are closely linked to improving the lives of poorer people and giving everyone an equal chance.

Goals 4 and 5 aim to improve the health and life of mothers and children.

Bold targets

Each goal has targets that need to be achieved by the year 2015, and governments have been asked to make policies to ensure these targets are met. The targets for goals 4 and 5 are as follows:

• to reduce the number of children dying before the age of five by two thirds;

• to reduce the number of women dying in pregnancy and childbirth by 75 per cent.

THE EIGHT MILLENNIUM DEVELOPMENT GOALS

1 Get rid of extreme poverty and hunger

2 Primary education for all

3 Promote equal chances for girls and women

4 Reduce child mortality

5 Improve the health of mothers

6 Combat HIV/AIDS, malaria and other diseases

7 Ensure environmental sustainability

8 Address the special needs of developing countries, including debt and fair trade

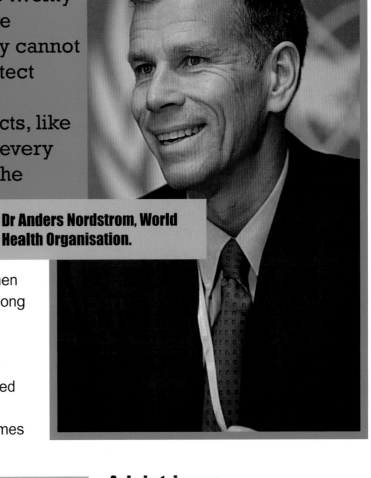

> ❝ It is unacceptable, in the twenty-first century, that children are disabled or die because they cannot access the vaccines that protect them from polio, measles or pneumonia. But some products, like some soft drinks, make it to every village in the world. What's the difference? ❞

Dr Anders Nordstrom, World Health Organisation.

Simple solutions?

Most experts agree that a great many women and children could be set on the road to a long and healthy life with a few basic changes. These include training more midwives, educating mothers in basic health, hygiene and family planning issues, using special bed nets to prevent the spread of malaria and adopting worldwide immunisation programmes against diseases such as measles.

▲ **Women and children collect fresh spring water in a village in Ethiopia.**

A joint issue

The Millennium Development Goals recognise that the health of mothers and the health of children cannot in fact be separated. Healthy mothers are more likely to have a successful pregnancy, they are more likely to breastfeed their newborn babies and are more likely to provide a plentiful, balanced diet for their children. They are also more likely to seek medical help in the form of immunisations or medicines for their children.

? **Can you think of any links between Millennium Development Goals 4 and 5 and the other six Goals?**

Government action

Disease, hunger, poverty, lack of education – these problems put the lives of mothers, babies and young children at risk. Yet as the Millennium Development Goals suggest, all of these problems can be overcome and millions of lives can be saved if countries work together to bring about change.

What rich countries can do

Rich countries, supported by their governments, can provide health experts, medicines, equipment and food to those parts of the world that need them most. They can provide money for more health clinics, hospitals and feeding centres. Rich countries can also invest in research into new vaccines and treatments, and then ensure that they are made available and affordable for all.

Mrs Chamutsa's family has received help with food and shelter from overseas donors such as the European Commission and the British government.

What poor countries can do

The governments of poor countries can work to ensure that any aid arriving from richer countries is distributed fairly and made available to everyone. They can implement real solutions such as educating people about how to stay healthy, overseeing national immunisation programmes and training more health workers. They can also work to remove the prejudices that result in some pregnant women being denied access to proper health care by their husbands and families.

Mass immunisation

Mass immunisation programmes are the most effective way to deal with specific diseases such as polio, rubella and measles. In 2007 UNICEF (United Nations Children's Fund) began working with the government of the Democratic People's Republic of Korea to immunise all its children against measles in an effort to rid the country of this disease once and for all.

Gopalan Balagopal of UNICEF Korea says:

" Measles is highly contagious, but completely preventable. For this campaign to be successful we must ensure that every child is properly vaccinated. "

Changing attitudes

Bringing about change is not just about providing money, food and medicines. It is also about improving the status of women in their communities and ensuring equal access to healthcare. For example, when governments promote family planning services, women are more likely to have a bigger gap between babies which is better for them and better for their children. It also means that they are more likely to protect themselves against sexually transmitted diseases such as HIV/AIDS.

 This child has the HIV virus. It was passed to him from his mother before he was even born. If women can learn how to protect themselves from the virus then their children would be protected too.

? ■ What would you like your government to do to reduce the number of children dying each day throughout the world?

Local solutions

There are all sorts of reasons why mothers and young children are especially vulnerable to illness and disease. Problems such as hunger or poverty are common in many countries, but sometimes the best way to defeat them is to look carefully at the needs of a particular village or region. Aid organisations around the world work with local groups to find lasting solutions.

Children in Crisis is working in partnership with local organisation Jinpa to train midwives in Tibet. This woman is learning how to hold a baby correctly. A spokesman for Children in Crisis says:

" The women of today will be the mothers of the future generation; saving a child is like saving a hope for the future. "

Training for midwives in China

For people living in a remote area of China called Yushu, access to clinics and doctors is almost impossible. Women have little knowledge of pregnancy and lack basic information about how an infection spreads. However, now the charity Children in Crisis is working in partnership with a local organisation called Jinpa to train young women to be midwives. When the midwives finish their training they return to their local communities to look after new mothers and babies and teach families about hygiene and first aid.

A young girl helped by the organisation Jinpa.

Vitamin supplements for Darany Heang

Darany Heang's family eats porridge and in the rainy season they catch fish and harvest rice. However, this is not a balanced diet. It does not contain enough essential vitamins and minerals.

When Darany Heang's sight was affected, his parents did not realise that this was due to a lack of green vegetables and fruit in his diet. Fortunately he was discovered by a local community development organisation sponsored by UNICEF.

A UNICEF spokesman says:

" Now we have discovered Darany Heang, he is receiving treatment for his vitamin A deficiency and his progress is monitored by outreach workers from the local health centre. **"**

▲ A woman collects pulses at a feeding centre.

A feeding programme in Bangladesh

The soil is very poor in Nasha Rana's village in Bangladesh. It is difficult to grow vegetables, so a local organisation teaches families to gather wild vegetables. They also run a feeding centre where Nasha's 14-month-old daughter Saba is given a carefully balanced mix of pulses, fruits, vegetables and oils. Nasha says that if Saba was not given this she would have only rice and salt to eat. Now, Nasha and Saba are putting on weight and they haven't been ill for a while.

? Why is it important to have local knowledge about a community in order to help the people who live there?

People who help

People who help to save the lives of women and young children around the world come from many different backgrounds. Sometimes experts travel to poorer or more remote parts of the world to share their knowledge with others. Sometimes people work within their own communities as midwives or health educators. All are trying to make sure that young families can survive and flourish.

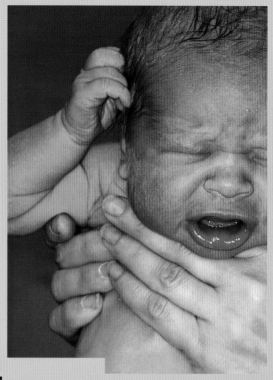

Cathy Ellis helps midwives in Kosovo look after new babies.

" Even though we can't speak the language, they know we care about them and they make it clear that they really appreciate it. **"**

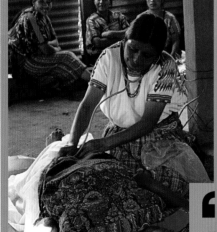

Heidy says:

Midwives

Cathy Ellis is a midwife from Canada who trains new midwives in Kosovo. She says she is motivated to help the Kosovar women have safe and happy births.

In Guatemala, Heidy's grandmother Marta never hesitates when an expectant mother in their village needs her help.

" The work my grandmother does is really important. Even if there is a family get-together, if she has commitments at church, if it is raining or night-time, she is still prepared to run and help. **"**

Health workers

Jhorna Rai is a health worker who runs six feeding centres in Bangladesh. These centres monitor childrens' weight and height to see if they are malnourished, and provide health education for mothers.

Jhorna Rai says:

" Every day I call on the mothers to speak to them. I advise them to keep their food clean and eat more vegetables. I was trained in nutrition by CCDB (Christian Commission for Development in Bangladesh) and I have a diploma in nursing. "

Family carers

Levels of child malnutrition are high in Ica, Peru. Many children have to look after younger siblings while their parents work in poorly paid jobs. Ten-year-old Angelica goes to school, works in a pharmacy and looks after her baby sister Dayana. With Christian Aid partner IEME (the Spanish Institute of Foreign Missions), she is learning about the foods she and her sister can eat to keep them well, and learning exercises to stimulate her sister.

" I give Dayana massages and we do exercises. I show her flashcards with pictures of things on them and a word. She likes it, she laughs and claps when we do it. She learns things, I think she is going to be very clever. "

Angelica speaks about caring for her sister.

? What do Cathy Ellis, Marta, Jhorna Rai and Angelica have in common?

Support for new mothers

Children stand a much better chance in life if their mothers are healthy, know how to care for their children and are willing to speak up for themselves and their families. Pregnant women and new mothers can be helped and supported in so many different ways, from health care and aid to education and training.

Isabel Sardinas is one of the mothers who has taken part in a scheme in Bolivia to help mothers during pregnancy. She says:

❝ Before we hardly went to the doctor to be treated. Now we can go because they treat us as if we were in our own houses, and we can have our husbands and a midwife by our sides. **❞**

Listening to mothers

In one area of Bolivia, local women felt misunderstood by doctors and so were reluctant to attend clinics during their pregnancies. As a result, many women were dying in childbirth. Causananchispaj (which means "to be able to live") worked with local health clinics to make sure they listened to the concerns of pregnant women and allowed them to make their own choices about their health care and giving them the confidence to attend clinics. As a result, the number of women dying in childbirth fell dramatically.

Educating mothers

Nurse Joyce Kaoza is a child survival nurse at a clinic for mothers and babies in Malawi. As well as weighing and assessing the babies she holds monthly health education classes for the new mothers.

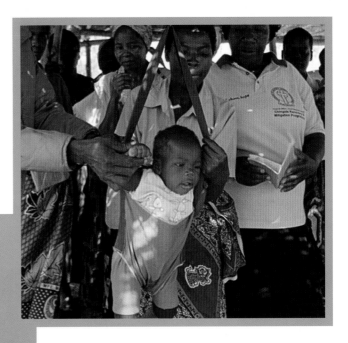

Joyce Kaoza says:

"Today they are asking about the difference between breast milk and powdered milk bought from a shop. We're explaining why breast milk is best. We also teach them how to prepare a healthy meal, for example how to make porridge with mixed in tomatoes or eggs and crushed fish. "

Saba's mother Nasha is quite clear about the value of all she has learned from the Christian Commission for Development in Bangladesh.

Nasha says:

"Every day I call on the mothers to speak to them. I know how to advise them to keep their food clean and eat more vegetables. This is because I was trained in nutrition a local group. I am so happy I have these skills now, as it means I can help others as well as Saba. "

? Nasha Rana has learned about the importance of good hygiene. In what way will this be good for the rest of her community?

Giving families hope

All around the world, mothers, babies and young children are being helped, often in very simple ways, towards longer, healthier lives. Basic things like clean water, medicine, food or the presence of a nurse or midwife give families hope for the future.

Darany's mother says:

" Now we know Darany's problem can be treated we are very happy. We know he will not get better straight away but soon maybe he will be able to play and study more with his brothers and sister and when he's older he can lead a better life. "

Treating the problem
When Darany Heang was given Vitamin A drops, his eyesight began to improve significantly. His mother is now very hopeful.

Mrs Chamutsa's granddaughter Gladys is now being helped to go to school where she is studying for her exams.

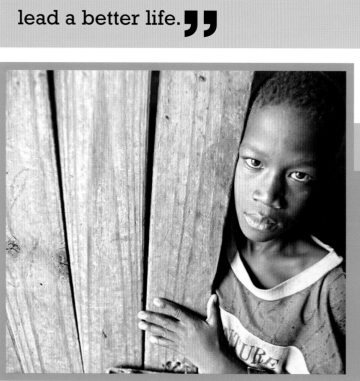

Gladys says:

" Life is a constant struggle. I have to work before and after school, but I am just grateful me and my siblings are in school - this way tomorrow may be better than today. "

At last Nasha can see a future for her daughter.

" I hope that I can send Saba to school. **"**

A brighter future

Thanks to the infant feeding programme attended by Saba and her mother Nasha, Saba is getting stronger every day. Nasha is determined that Saba should enjoy a brighter future and get an education.

" I am very proud to have a grandmother who helps so many people. **"**

Gladys is very proud about what her grandmother has done for her family.

? How is your life different to that of Darany Heang, Gladys Chamutsa, Nasha and Saba, and Heidy? How is it the same?

Action you can take

More than 10 million children are still dying each year in the developing world. Vaccination programmes, feeding centres and clinics, the provision of insecticide-treated bed nets and better education about health and hygiene are all helping to reduce this figure, but there is still a tremendous amount of work to be done and everyone can help.

▲ Write a letter to your member of parliament, asking them to keep the promises they made.

Make your voice heard

One hundred and ninety one governments around the world have signed up to the Millennium Development Goals. You can write to your country's leaders to ask them how they intend to keep the promises they have made to stop mothers and children from dying of preventable diseases. What action are they taking?

Hold an awareness assembly

Put on a special assembly at your school to highlight some of the issues about child health around the world. You could act out the first years of a child born in a poor country, who is malnourished and has no access to medical services. Contrast this with the first years of a child born in a wealthy country. Show what happens to each child when they become ill.

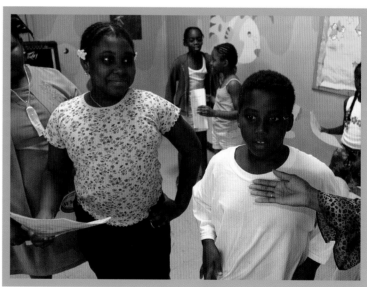

▲ Act out a play highlighting the problems facing children born in the developing world.

We believe in life before death

Support a charity

There are many charities that work to improve the health of mothers and children. Research the work of organisations such as UNICEF, Save the Children and Christian Aid and decide how you would like to help. Request a schools information pack where available and start raising money. Save the Children (www.savethechildren.org) have a great list of fun ways to do this.

Design a poster

Many people don't know that a very small amount of money can save the life of a young child. Make a poster for your school or church or community building to show the following:

Every day:

2,000 children die from measles

Cost of a preventative vaccine – 50 pence

4,000 children die from diarrhoea

Cost of a packet of life-saving oral rehydration salts – 5 pence

And every day only two per cent of African children sleep under a treated bed net which protects against malaria

Cost of a treated bed net – £1.50

WE CAN AFFORD TO SAVE LIVES

▲ The official logo of the charity Christian Aid, who help poor children around the world, whatever their religion.

▲ A young mother and her child receive the care they deserve at a baby clinic in Nigeria.

? **How will you help to achieve the Millennium Development Goals?**

Glossary

Aid money, food and resources sent to help those who need it

Anti-retroviral drugs drugs that can slow the development of HIV/AIDS in an infected person

Balanced diet a healthy mix of fruit, vegetables, protein and carbohydrate

Dehydrated severe lack of water

Developing countries poorer countries

Diarrhoea a stomach bug, often caused by poor hygiene

Diet what we eat

Family planning learning how to plan your pregnancy and how to avoid some of the health risks associated with having too many babies

Formula milk milk for babies with added vitamins and minerals

Hygiene level of cleanliness

HIV/AIDS a disease which attacks the body's natural immune system

Immunisation an injection or medicine that stops us getting certain diseases

Insecticide treated bed net a net sprayed with the chemicals that kill mosquitoes which is hung over beds to protect people while they sleep

Malaria a serious disease spread by mosquitoes in hot, humid countries

Malnutrition severe lack of food

Midwife someone trained to look after mothers and babies before, during and after birth

Mortality number of deaths

Nutrients food elements essential for health and growth such as vitamins, minerals and protein

Pre-eclampsia a condition that can be very dangerous for pregnant women if it is not treated

Prejudice an unfair view of someone

Preventable deaths deaths which can be prevented with the right treatment

Resources things people need, such as money, food, materials and medicines

Sterilised made free from germs

Find out more

Useful websites

www.un.org/cyberschoolbus
Go to the Millennium Development Goals for accessible and child-friendly facts about the MDGs. Also useful for information about the work of the United Nations.

www.millenniumcampaign.org/goals_poverty
Go to www.millenniumcampaign.org <http://www.millenniumcampaign.org and click on Goals 4 and 5 to find the latest news, facts and statistics as well as information about what you can do to help ensure the health of mothers and children around the world. For children aged 11 and over, go to: www.millenniumcampaign.org Click on "Who's Doing What" then "Youth", and download the Youth Action Guide.

Note to parents and teachers:
Every effort has been made by the Publishers to ensure that these websites are suitable for children, that they are of the highest educational value, and that they contain no inappropriate or offensive material. However, because of the nature of the Internet, it is impossible to guarantee that the contents of these sites will not be altered. We strongly advise that Internet access is supervised by a responsible adult.

www.careinternational.org.uk
Click on "What we do" then "Health," then "Saving mothers' lives" to find out how one organisation is helping women in Guatemala.

www.rehydrate.org
This site contains lots of facts and statistics about the dangers of dehydration for mothers and children.

Christian Aid websites

Christian Aid contributed one of the real-life stories in this book (the accounts of Heidy and her gran) and the stories about Angelica and Dayana, and Asirene Magalasi. You can find out more about this organisation by following the links below:

www.christianaid.org.uk
The main site for the charity Christian Aid, who help disadvantaged children and adults all over the world, regardless of their religion.

www.globalgang.org.uk
Christian Aid's website for kids with games, news and stories from around the world.

Index